To:

_____

From:

_____

Published by Simple Truths
1952 McDowell Road, Suite 300
Naperville, Illinois 60563

Book Design: Brian Frantz

Simple Truths is a registered trademark.
Printed and bound in the United States of America

800-900-3427
www.simpletruths.com

ISBN 978-1-60810-134-4

02 WOZ 11

LEADERSHIP QUOTES

Compiled by
MAC ANDERSON

Introduction

I love quotes! Always have ... always will.

In fact, my love of quotes inspired me to publish my very first book, a small, 80-page quotation book that I called *Motivational Quotes*. I'm pleased to say it sold 800,000 copies.

That book covers quotations on a wide variety of topics, but as a lifetime entrepreneur, **I've always been fascinated by the topic of leadership**. What traits, or qualities, do most great leaders possess?

Thus, the inspiration for this book! My goal was to find the very best quotes on the most important traits of leadership...like **vision**, **passion**, **serving**, **integrity** and **commitment to excellence** ... to name a few.

Therefore, if you're a leader, or aspire to be a leader, it is my hope that *Leadership Quotes* will inspire you ... to inspire others.

Lead with Passion,

Mac Anderson
Founder, Simple Truths and Successories

The pessimist complains about the wind.

The optimist expects it to change.

The realist adjusts the sails.

William Arthur Ward

Leadership is the capacity

to **translate** vision into reality.

Warren G. Bennis

Management is doing things right.
Leadership is doing the right things.

Peter Drucker

Excellence is an art won by training and habituation.
We do not act rightly because we have **virtue** or excellence,
but rather we have those because we have acted rightly.
We are what we repeatedly do.

Excellence, then, is not an act but a habit.

Aristotle

One of the true tests of leadership
is the ability to recognize a problem
before it becomes an emergency.

Arnold H. Glasgow

Not everything that is faced can be changed.

But nothing can be changed until it is faced.

James Baldwin

Here is a simple but **powerful rule** –
always give people more than what they expect to get.

Nelson Boswell

◆ ◆ ◆ ◆ ◆

If you want to know why

your people are not performing well,

step up to the mirror and take a peek.

Ken Blanchard

The first responsibility of a leader is to define reality,

the last is to say "Thank you."

In **between** the two,

the leader must become a servant.

Max De Pree

They don't care how much you know

until they know how much you care.

Theodore Roosevelt

Nothing so conclusively proves a man's ability to lead others as what he does from day to day to lead himself.

Thomas J. Watson

❖ ❖ ❖ ❖ ❖

The greatest management principle in the world is:

"the things that get rewarded

and appreciated get done."

Michael LeBoeuf

The price of leadership is **responsibility**.

Winston Churchill

Excellence is … Caring more than others think is wise;

Risking more than others think is safe;

Dreaming more than others think is practical.

Expecting more than others think is possible.

Winston Churchill

Y ou get the best efforts from others

not by lighting a fire beneath them,

but by **building a fire within**.

Bob Nelson

The supreme **quality** for a leader is unquestionably **integrity**.

Dwight D. Eisenhower

Integrity without **knowledge**

is weak and useless,

and **knowledge** without **integrity**

is dangerous and dreadful.

Samuel Johnson

Quality is never an accident:

It is always the result of high intention,

sincere **effort** , intelligent **direction** and skillful **execution**.

It represents the wise **choice** of many alternatives.

William A. Foster

Values are critical guides for making decisions.

When in doubt, they cut through the fog

like **a beacon** in the night.

Robert Townsend

The best executive is one who has sense enough to pick **good** people to do what he wants done, and **self-restraint** enough to keep from meddling with them while they do it.

Theodore Roosevelt

A leader's job is to look into the future

and see the organization not as it is,

but as it **should be.**

Jack Welch

◆ ◆ ◆ ◆ ◆

Giving people a little more than they expect

is a **good way** to get back

a lot more than you'd expect.

Robert Half

In looking for people to hire, you look for three qualities:

integrity, **intelligence**, and **energy**.

And if they don't have the first,

the other two will kill you.

Warren Buffett

The most important persuasion tool you have

in your entire arsenal is integrity.

Zig Ziglar

❖ ❖ ❖ ❖ ❖

To lead the people,

walk behind them.

Lao Tzu

People working together...

building, sharing, lifting, helping, encouraging...

can accomplish **anything**.

The final forming of a person's character

lies in their own hands.

Anne Frank

Though leadership may be hard to define,

the one characteristic common to all leaders

is the ability to **make things happen**.

Ted W. Engstrom

The ratio of "We's" to "I's" is the best indicator

of the development of a **team**.

Lewis B. Ergen

The quality of a person's life

is in direct proportion to their commitment to excellence,

regardless of their chosen field of endeavor.

Vince Lombardi

I think we all have a little voice inside us that will guide us if we shut out all the noise and clutter from our lives and **listen to that voice,** it will tell us **the right thing** to do.

Christopher Reeve

Integrity has no need of rules.

Albert Camus

No one can whistle a **symphony**.

It takes an **orchestra** to play it.

Halford E. Luccock

The gates of opportunity and advancement

swing on these **four hinges**:

initiative, **industry**, insight, and **integrity**.

William Arthur Ward

Leaders are leaders

because they are the greater servants.

The way **up** is **down**.

Francis M. Cosgrove, Jr.

If your actions inspire others to dream more,

learn more, do more, and become more,

you are a leader.

John Quincy Adams

Teamwork is the ability to work together

toward a **common vision**.

The ability to direct individual accomplishment

toward **organizational objectives**.

It is the fuel that allows common people

to attain **uncommon results**.

Andrew Carnegie

Individual **commitment** to a group effort –

that is what makes a team work,

a company work,

a society work,

a civilization work.

Vince Lombardi

◆ ◆ ◆ ◆ ◆

Example is not the main thing

in influencing others.

It is the only thing.

Albert Schweitzer

◆ ◆ ◆ ◆ ◆

Excellence is not a skill. **It is an attitude**.

Ralph Marston

There is only one boss.

The customer.

And he can fire everybody in the company

from the chairman on down,

simply by spending his money somewhere else.

Sam Walton

The task of a leader is two-fold:

to push us **toward** the rapids

and **away** from the rocks.

Ron Cole

You can do what I cannot do.

I can do what you cannot do.

Together we can do great things.

Mother Teresa

Leaders must be close enough to **relate** to others,

but far enough ahead to **motivate** them.

John C. Maxwell

◆ ◆ ◆ ◆ ◆

A gifted leader is one who is capable

of touching your heart.

Jacob Samuel Potofsky

Contrary to popular belief,

there most certainly is an "I" in "team."

It is the same "I" that appears

three times in "responsibility."

Amber Harding

Quality in a service or product is not what you put into it.

It is what the client or customer gets out of it.

Peter F. Drucker

Excellence is to do a common thing

in **an uncommon** way.

Booker T. Washington

A leader leads by **example** not by force.

Sun Tzu

Customer service is just a day-in, day-out ongoing,

never-ending, unremitting, persevering,

compassionate, type of activity.

Leon Gorman

Let unswerving integrity ever be your watchword.

Bernard M. Baruch

◆ ◆ ◆ ◆ ◆

A hundred thousand men coming one after another

could not move a ton weight,

but the **united strength** of fifty

would transport it with ease.

George Washington

In a way, leadership is as delicate as Mozart's melodies.

The music exists and it doesn't. It is written on the page,

but it means nothing until performed and heard.

Much of its effect depends on the performer

and the listener.

The best leaders, like the best music,

inspire us to see new possibilities.

Max De Pree

If you work just for money, you'll never make it,

but if you love what you're doing

and you always put the customer first,

success will be yours.

Ray Kroc

The secret of joy in work is contained in one word –

excellence.

To know how to do something well is to enjoy it.

Pearl Buck

❖ ❖ ❖ ❖ ❖

A leader has the **vision** and **conviction**

that a dream can be achieved.

He inspires the **power** and **energy** to get it done.

Ralph Nader

❖ ❖ ❖ ❖ ❖

If you have integrity, nothing else matters.

If you don't have integrity, nothing else matters.

Alan K. Simpson

◆ ◆ ◆ ◆ ◆

Whether you are big or small,

you cannot give good customer service

if your employees don't feel good

about coming to work.

Martin Oliver

You can have the world's greatest product,

backed up by the most magnificent business plan...

but if your people – from the telephone operator

to the CEO – aren't turned on,

and your customers aren't turned on,

forget it. It's all over. Period.

Tom Peters

❖ ❖ ❖ ❖ ❖

Every contact we have with a customer

influences whether or not they'll come back.

We have to be **great** every time or we'll lose them.

Kevin Stirtz

◆ ◆ ◆ ◆ ◆

Do what you do so well

that they will want to see it

again and bring their friends.

Walt Disney

Excellence is a better teacher than mediocrity.

The lessons of the **ordinary** are everywhere.

Truly profound and original insights are to be found

only in studying the **exemplary**.

Warren G. Bennis

You will never be a leader

unless you first learn to follow and be led.

Tiorio

❖ ❖ ❖ ❖ ❖

A group becomes a team when each

member is sure enough of himself

and his contribution to **praise the skills of the others**.

Norman Shidle

To me,

leading is learning,

and the moment you stop learning

you stop leading

and your organization stops growing.

Rick Warren

The single most important thing to remember

about any enterprise is that

there are no results inside its walls.

The result of a business

is a satisfied customer.

Peter F. Drucker

You will never become a **fine leader**

until you become a **fine servant**.

Ellie Lofaro

Integrity is one of several paths.

It distinguishes itself from the others

because it is the right path

and the only one on which

you will never get lost.

M.H. McKee

Desire is the key to motivation,

but it's determination and commitment

to an unrelenting pursuit of your goal—

a commitment to excellence—

that will enable you to attain **the success you seek**.

Mario Andretti

You've got to love your people more than your position.

John C. Maxwell

◆ ◆ ◆ ◆ ◆

Anyone who has achieved excellence in any form knows that it comes as a result of ceaseless concentration.

Louise Brooks

People acting together as a group

can accomplish things which

no individual acting alone

could ever hope to bring about.

Franklin Delano Roosevelt

Leaders need to be **optimists**.

Their **vision** is beyond the present.

Rudy Giuliani

◆ ◆ ◆ ◆ ◆

The very essence of leadership is that you have a vision.

It's got to be a vision you articulate

clearly and **forcefully** on every occasion.

You can't blow an uncertain trumpet.

Theodore Hesburgh

All winning teams are goal-oriented.

Teams like these win consistently because everyone

connected with them concentrates on specific objectives.

They go about their business with blinders on;

nothing will distract them from achieving their aims.

Lou Holtz

Set your expectations high;

find men and women whose

integrity and values you respect;

get their agreement on a course of action;

and give them your ultimate trust.

John Akers

❖ ❖ ❖ ❖ ❖

Some people have greatness thrust upon them.

Few have excellence thrust upon them ... they achieve it.

They do not achieve it unwittingly by doing what

comes naturally and they don't stumble into it in the

course of amusing themselves.

All excellence involves discipline and tenacity of purpose.

John W. Gardner

Effective leaders do not accept this feeling of defeat

because they know how disempowering it is.

Without heart, there can be no passion,

no enthusiasm, no feeling of energy and no charisma.

A leader high on heart

and emotional intelligence breeds victory.

A disheartened leader,

doubtful and stressed, manifests loss.

John J. Murphy

❖ ❖ ❖ ❖ ❖

W hen a team outgrows individual performance

and learns **team confidence,**

excellence becomes a reality.

Joe Paterno

A im for **service** and **success** will follow.

Albert Schweitzer

It is simply service that measures **success**.

George Washington Carver

❖ ❖ ❖ ❖ ❖

Leadership is **action**, not position.

Donald H. McGannon

Striving for **excellence** motivates you;

striving for **perfection** is demoralizing.

Harriet Beryl Braiker

◆ ◆ ◆ ◆ ◆

Perhaps the most central characteristic

of authentic **leadership** is the relinquishing

of the impulse to dominate others.

David Cooper

And **then some** … these three little words are the secret to success.

They are the difference between average people

and top people in most companies.

The top people always do what is expected … **and then some**.

They are thoughtful of others,

they are considerate and kind … **and then some**.

They meet their responsibilities fairly and square … **and then some**.

They are good friends and helpful neighbors … **and then some**.

They can be counted on in an emergency … **and then some**.

I am thankful for people like this,

for they make the world a better place.

Their spirit of service is summed up in these three little words …

and then some.

Carl Holmes

❖ ❖ ❖ ❖ ❖

The foundation of teamwork is built on these things:

respect, **trust**, and a **common goal**.

If we don't take care of our customers,

somebody else will.

Unknown

◆ ◆ ◆ ◆ ◆

Excellence is doing **ordinary** things **extraordinarily** well.

John W. Gardner

No man will make a great leader

who wants to do it all himself,

or get all the credit for doing it.

Andrew Carnegie

A man is only a leader

when a follower **stands beside him**.

Mark Brouwer

❖ ❖ ❖ ❖ ❖

P aint a masterpiece daily.

Always **autograph your work** with excellence.

Greg Hickman

Live so that when your children

think of **fairness** and **integrity,**

they think of you.

H. Jackson Brown, Jr.

Talent wins games, but teamwork

and intelligence wins championships.

Michael Jordan

No man ever reached to **excellence** in any one art or profession without having passed through the slow and painful process of study and preparation.

Horace

❖ ❖ ❖ ❖ ❖

The task of the leader is to get his people from where they are to where they have not been.

Henry Kissinger

Alone we can do **so little**,

together we can do **so much**.

Helen Keller

◆ ◆ ◆ ◆ ◆

Attitudes are contagious.

Is yours worth catching?

Unknown

Leaders don't create followers,

they create more leaders.

Tom Peters

A customer is the most important visitor on our premises.

He is not dependent on us … we are dependent on him.

He is not an outsider in our business—he is a part of it.

We are not doing him a favor by serving him …

he is doing us a favor by giving us
the opportunity to do so.

Unknown

◆ ◆ ◆ ◆ ◆

The growth and development of people

is the highest calling of **leadership**.

Harvey S. Firestone

Excellence just doesn't happen,

it must be **forged**, **tested** and **used**.

It must be passed downward into the very fabric

of our soul until it becomes our nature.

General Charles C. Krulack

The purpose of a business is to create
a mutually beneficial relationship
between itself and those that it serves.
When it does that well,
it will be around tomorrow to do it some more.

John Woods

Leaders are pioneers.

They are people who venture into unexplored territory.

They guide us to new and often unfamiliar destinations.

People who take the lead are foot soldiers

in the campaigns for change … the unique reason for

having leaders—their differentiating function—

is to move us forward.

Leaders get us going someplace.

James M. Kouzes

◆ ◆ ◆ ◆ ◆

Just make up your mind at the very outset

that your work is going to stand for **quality** ...

that you are going to stamp a superior quality

upon everything that goes out of your hands,

that whatever you do shall bear

the hallmark of excellence.

Orison Swett Marden

When everyone on the team is **accountable**,

the team's effectiveness rises above the sum of its parts.

Each team member does not just do what is asked,

but what is needed.

John H. Murphy

Of a good leader, who talks little,

when his work is done,

his aim fulfilled, they will say,

"We did this ourselves."

Lao-tzu

There are no excellent companies.

The old saying "If it ain't broke, don't fix it" needs revision.

I propose: "If it ain't broke,

you just haven't looked hard enough."

Fix it anyway.

Tom Peters

The strength of the **team**

is each individual member...

the strength of each member is the **team**.

Phil Jackson

It is easier to find a score of men wise enough

to discover the truth than to find one intrepid enough,

in the face of opposition, to stand up for it.

A.A. Hodge

◆ ◆ ◆ ◆ ◆

A leader's role is to raise people's aspirations

for what they can become

and to release their energies

so they will try to get there.

David Gergen

If you are going to achieve excellence in big things,

you develop the habit in little matters.

Excellence is not an exception,

it is a prevailing attitude.

Colin Powell

To give real service you must add something

which cannot be bought or measured with money,

and that is **sincerity** and **integrity**.

Donald N. Adams

❖ ❖ ❖ ❖ ❖

Customers will forget what you say,

but **they won't forget** how you made them feel.

Unknown

♦ ♦ ♦ ♦ ♦

I am a member of a team and I rely on the team.

I defer to it and sacrifice for it, because the team,

not the individual, is the **ultimate champion**.

Mia Hamm

82

A leader, once convinced

a particular course of action is the right one,

must have the determination to stick with it

and be undaunted when

the going gets rough.

Ronald Reagan

Don't worry so much about your self-esteem.

Worry more about your **character**.

Integrity is its own reward.

Dr. Laura Schlessinger

Appreciate everything your associates do for the business.

Nothing else can quite substitute for a few well-chosen,

well-timed, sincere **words of praise**.

They're absolutely free and worth a fortune.

Sam Walton

Good leaders must **become**

what they want their followers to become.

Nido R. Qubein

Customer service is not a department … **It's an attitude**.

Mac Anderson

No person can be a great leader unless he takes **genuine**

joy in the successes of those under him.

W.A. Nance

True leadership

must be for the benefit of the followers,

not the enrichment of the leaders.

Robert Townsend

You are already of consequence in the world if you are

known as a man of strict integrity.

If you can be absolutely relied upon;

if when you say a thing is so, it is so;

if when you say you will do a thing, you do it;

then you carry with you a passport to universal esteem.

Grenville Kleiser

Unity is strength...

where there is **teamwork** and **collaboration**,

wonderful things can be achieved.

Mattie Stepanek

In the end, all business operations
can be reduced to three words:
people, **product** and **profits**.
Unless you've got a good team,
you can't do much with the other two.

Lee Iacocca

It takes **months** to gain a customer...

only seconds to lose them.

Unknown

What is right is often **forgotten**

by what is convenient.

Bodie Thoene

The difference between

ordinary and **extraordinary**

is that little "extra."

Jimmy Johnson

♦ ♦ ♦ ♦ ♦

A leader is **best** when people

barely know that he exists.

Lao Tzu

Light is the task where many share the toil.

Homer

Integrity begins with a person being willing to be honest with himself.

Cort R. Flint

The difference between a successful person

and others is not a lack of **strength**,

not a lack of **knowledge**,

but a lack of **will**.

Vince Lombardi

Businesses planned for service are apt to **succeed**; businesses planned for profit are apt to fail.

Nicholas Murray Butler

✦ ✦ ✦ ✦ ✦

Leadership is not something you do **to** people; it's something you do **with** people.

Ken Blanchard

Outstanding leaders go out of their way

to boost the **self-esteem** of their personnel.

If people believe in themselves,

it's **amazing** what they can accomplish.

Sam Walton

◆ ◆ ◆ ◆ ◆

The path to **greatness** is along with others.

Baltasar Gracian

Companies don't succeed ... **people do**.

Mac Anderson

◆ ◆ ◆ ◆ ◆

One measure of leadership

is the **caliber** of people

who choose to **follow** you.

Dennis A. Peer

Integrity is not a conditional word.

It doesn't blow in the wind or **change** with the weather.

It is your inner **image** of yourself, and if you look in there

and see a man who won't cheat,

then you know he never will.

John D. MacDonald

A team is a group of people who
may not be equal in experience,
talent or education but in **commitment**.

Patricia Fripp

◆ ◆ ◆ ◆ ◆

Our greatest danger in life

is in permitting the urgent things

to crowd out the **important**.

Charles Hummel

Being on par in terms of price and quality
only gets you into the game.
Service wins the game.

Tony Alessandra

◆ ◆ ◆ ◆ ◆

Dreams get you started …

discipline keeps you going.

Jim Rohn

Courage is …

Sacrificing personal gain

for the benefit of others;

Speaking your mind

even though others don't agree;

Taking complete responsibility

for your **actions** and your mistakes.

Doing what you know is right— regardless of the consequences.

Eric Harvey

❖ ❖ ❖ ❖ ❖

The crux of leadership is that you must constantly stop to consider how your **decisions** will **influence** people.

Michigan State Police Maxim

Right is right, even if everyone is against it;

and **wrong is wrong**, even if everyone is for it.

William Penn

◆ ◆ ◆ ◆ ◆

A leader is a dealer in **hope**.

Napoleon Bonaparte

It's simple ... go the **extra mile**

and you will stand out from the crowd.

Robin Crow

The ultimate measure of a man

is not where he stands in moments

of comfort and convenience,

but where he stands at time

of challenge and controversy.

Martin Luther King, Jr.

A leader is not an administrator who loves to run others,

but someone who carries water for his people

so they can get on with their jobs.

Robert Townsend

People with **integrity** do

what they say they are going to do.

Others have excuses.

Dr. Laura Schlessinger

The only thing that stands between a person

and what they want from life is often

the will to **try it** and the **faith to believe** it's possible.

Richard M. DeVos

A life lived with **integrity**—

even if it lacks the trappings of fame and fortune—

is a **shining star** in whose light

others may follow in the years to come.

Denis Waitley

Real leadership is not about prestige, power or status.
It's about taking complete **responsibility**
for an organization's **well-being** and **growth**,
and changing it for the better.

Robert L. Joss

❖ ❖ ❖ ❖ ❖

Don't bother just to be better

than your contemporaries or predecessors.

Try to be **better** than yourself.

William Faulkner

If a man's associates find him guilty of phoniness,

if they find that he lacks forthright integrity, he will fail.

His teachings and actions must square with each other.

The first great need, therefore,

is integrity and high purpose.

Dwight D. Eisenhower

We cannot get what we've never had,

unless we're willing to do what we've never done.

Brian Tracy

Strive for excellence, not perfection.

H. Jackson Brown, Jr.

A leader is one

who sees more than others see,

who sees farther than others see,

and who sees before others do.

Leroy Eims

◆ ◆ ◆ ◆ ◆

The true measure of your character

is what you would do

if you were sure no one would ever find out.

John C. Maxwell

Integrity is the rock upon which we build

our business success—

our quality products and services,

our forthright relations with customers and suppliers,

and ultimately, our winning competitive record.

GE's quest for competitive excellence begins

and ends with our commitment to ethical conduct.

Jack Welch, Chairman of General Electric

Leadership is the art of getting someone else

to do something you want done,

because he wants to do it.

Dwight D. Eisenhower

Your success in any business will always be in direct

proportion to your ability to consistently exceed

expectations of your customers.

Robin Crow

112

Be willing to make decisions.

That's the most important quality of a good leader.

Don't fall victim to what I call

the ready-aim-aim-aim syndrome.

You must be willing to fire.

T. Boone Pickens

❖ ❖ ❖ ❖ ❖

To measure a leader,

put a tape around his heart, not his head.

John C. Maxwell

Coming together is a **beginning**.

Keeping together is **progress**.

Working together is **success**.

James Crook

◆ ◆ ◆ ◆ ◆

A man who wants to lead the orchestra

must turn his back on the crowd.

James Crook

Those who can command themselves,

command others.

William Hazlitt

A great leader **never** sets himself above his followers

except in carrying responsibilities.

Jules Ormont

The key elements in the art of working together

are how to deal with **change** and how to deal with

conflict … the needs of the team are best met when we

meet the needs of individual persons.

Max De Pree

A true leader has the confidence to stand alone,

the courage to make tough decisions

and the compassion to listen to the needs of others.

They are much like eagles ... They don't flock,

you find them one at a time.

M.H. McKee

In the race for quality there is **no** finish line.

Mac Anderson

Excellence is the gradual result

of always striving to do better.

Pat Riley

Great leadership usually starts with a willing **heart**,

a positive **attitude**,

and a desire to **make a difference**.

Mac Anderson

◆ ◆ ◆ ◆ ◆

Wisdom is knowing the right path to take.

Integrity is taking it.

M.H. McKee

◆ ◆ ◆ ◆ ◆

In matters of principle,

stand like a rock;

in matters of taste,

swim with the current.

Thomas Jefferson

The attitude of the leader

will determine the attitude of the pack.

Integrity is not what we do as much as who we are.

And who we are, in turn,

determines what we do.

John Maxwell

Be a yardstick of quality.

Some people aren't used to an environment where

excellence is expected.

Steve Jobs

We see our customers as invited guests to a party,
and we are the hosts. It's our job every day
to make every important aspect of
the customer experience a little bit better.

Jeff Bezos

Integrity does not blow in the wind

or change with the tide.

It is the inner image of our true selves.

There's no straighter road to success

than exceeding expectations one day at a time.

Robin Crow

A good leader inspires people

to have confidence in their leader.

A great leader inspires people

to have confidence in themselves.

Lao Tzu

Success doesn't happen by accident.

It starts with an unwavering commitment

to build a dedicated team

who serves their boss ... **the customer**.

Mac Anderson

❖ ❖ ❖ ❖ ❖

Again and again, the impossible problem

is **solved** when we see that the problem is only

a tough decision waiting to be made.

Robert H. Schuller

No one will question your **integrity**

if your integrity is not questionable.

Nathaniel Bronner Jr.

◆ ◆ ◆ ◆ ◆

Leadership is a matter of having people look at you
and gain confidence, seeing how you react.
If you're in control, they're in control.

Tom Landry

You must be careful how you walk,

and where you go, for there are those following you

who will set their feet where yours are set.

Robert E. Lee

♦ ♦ ♦ ♦ ♦

Build for your team a feeling of oneness,

of dependence on one another

and of strength to be derived by unity.

Vincent Lombardi

Cooperation is the thorough conviction that nobody can get there unless **everybody** gets there.

Virginia Burden

Never doubt that a small group of committed people

can **change** the world.

Indeed, it is the only thing that ever has.

Margaret Mead

Successful leaders embrace the power of teamwork

by tapping into the innate **strengths**

each person brings to the table.

Scott Beare

❖ ❖ ❖ ❖ ❖

Leaders aren't born, they are made.

They are made by hard **effort**,

which is the price which all of us

must pay to achieve

any goal which is worthwhile.

Vince Lombardi

Everyone wants to feel that the hours that they spend every day at work **matter**, so let your team members know the value of their contributions in making your business a SUCCESS.

Peter Drucker

Real leaders are ordinary people with extraordinary determination.

John Seaman Garns

Real integrity is doing the right thing,

knowing that nobody's going to know

whether you did it or not.

Oprah Winfrey

People ask the difference in a leader and a boss.

The leader **leads** and the boss **drives**.

Theodore Roosevelt

Your most unhappy customers

are your greatest **source** of learning.

Bill Gates

Leaders are **visionaries** with a poorly developed sense

of fear and no concept of the odds against them.

Robert Jarvik

Bees accomplish nothing save as they **work together**,

and neither do men.

Auguste Comte

◆ ◆ ◆ ◆ ◆

Excellence demands **competition**.

Without a race there can be no champion,

no records broken, no excellence—

in education or in any other walk of life.

Ronald Reagan

If everyone is moving forward together,

then **success** will take care of itself.

Henry Ford

Give a man a fish and you feed him for a day.

Teach a man to fish and you feed him for a **lifetime**.

Chinese proverb

My grandfather once told me

that there are two kinds of people:

those who work and those who take the credit.

He told me to try to be in the first group;

there was less competition there.

Indira Gandhi

The real **leader** has no need to lead -
he is content to point the way.

Henry Miller

Integrity is not a ninety percent thing,

not a ninety-five percent thing.

Either you have it or you don't.

Peter Scotese

Everyone can be great ... because everyone can serve.

Dr. Martin Luther King, Jr.

◆ ◆ ◆ ◆ ◆

Successes have many fathers, failures have none.

Philip Caldwell

Keeping our employees as satisfied as our customers

is the key to excellent service.

Jack Baraona

Leadership is high touch.

It is grounded in the four chambers of leadership's heart:

intimacy, integrity, passion and competence.

John C. Maxwell

Technology, buildings, balance sheets and all the elements we think of as making up the essentials of business must **support** the central theme of doing something for someone.

Jack Falvey

To know what to do is **wisdom**.

To know how to do is **skill**.

To do the thing as it should be done is service.

Most of us are wise and skillful,

but it's service that prospers—service.

Charlie "Tremendous" Jones

If you wonder what getting and keeping

the right employees has to do with getting and keeping

the right customers, the answer is everything.

Fred Reichheld

❖ ❖ ❖ ❖ ❖

The best leaders ... almost without exception

and at every level,

are master users of stories and symbols.

Thomas J. Peters

The nice thing about **teamwork**

is that you always have others on your side.

Margaret Carty

◆ ◆ ◆ ◆ ◆

Leadership is getting someone to do

what they don't want to do,

to **achieve** what they want to achieve.

Tom Landry

${\rm M}$anagement is efficient

in climbing the ladder of **success**;

leadership determines whether

the ladder is leaning against the right wall.

Stephen R. Covey

A man who wants to lead the orchestra

must turn his back on the crowd.

Max Lucado

◆ ◆ ◆ ◆ ◆

None of us is as **smart** as all of us.

Ken Blanchard

146

It is the responsibility of leadership

to provide opportunity,

and the responsibility of individuals to contribute.

William Pollard

❖ ❖ ❖ ❖ ❖

There is no such thing as a minor lapse of integrity.

Tom Peters

You can't lead anyone else further

than you have gone yourself.

Gene Mauch

❖ ❖ ❖ ❖ ❖

There are **countless** ways of attaining greatness,

but any road to reaching one's maximum potential

must be built on a bedrock of **respect** for the individual,

a **commitment** to excellence,

and a rejection of mediocrity.

Buck Rodgers

Teamwork is no accident.

It is the by-product of good leadership.

John Adair

The only correct actions are those

that demand no explanation and no apology.

Red Auerbach

Remember, upon the **conduct** of each

depends the **fate** of all.

Alexander the Great

◆ ◆ ◆ ◆ ◆

Success without **honor** is an unseasoned dish;

it will satisfy your hunger,

but won't taste good.

Joe Paterno

A successful leader **has** to be innovative.

If you're not one step ahead of the crowd,

you'll soon be a step behind everyone else.

John C. Maxwell

It is easier to cope with a bad conscience

than with a bad reputation.

Friedrich Nietzsche

◆ ◆ ◆ ◆ ◆

Remember the difference between a boss and a leader;

a boss says "**Go!**" - a leader says "**Let's go!**"

E.M. Kelly

Integrity is the essence of everything successful.

Richard Buckminster Fuller

◆ ◆ ◆ ◆ ◆

Excellence is in the details.

Give attention to the **details** and excellence will come.

Perry Paxton

◆ ◆ ◆ ◆ ◆

Character is much easier **kept** than recovered.

Thomas Paine

E**xcellence** means when a man or woman

asks of himself more than others do.

Jose Ortega y Gasset

A **good objective of leadership** is to help those

who are doing poorly to do well

and to help those who are doing well to do even better.

Jim Rohn

Make the workmanship surpass the materials.

Ovid

❖❖❖❖❖

To be successful,

you have to have your heart in your business,

and your business in your heart.

Thomas Watson, Sr.

Too many people think only of their own profit.

But business opportunity seldom knocks on the door

of self-centered people.

No customer ever goes to

a store merely to please the storekeeper.

Kazuo Inamori

Leadership is practiced not so much in words as in **attitude** and in **actions**.

Harold S. Geneen

◆ ◆ ◆ ◆ ◆

People are like sticks of dynamite...

the power is on the **inside**,

but **nothing happens until the fuse gets lit**.

Mac Anderson

About the Author

MAC ANDERSON is the founder of Simple Truths and Successories, Inc., the leader in designing and marketing products for motivation and recognition. These companies, however, are not the first success stories for Mac. He was also the founder and CEO of McCord Travel, the largest travel company in the Midwest, and part owner/VP of sales and marketing for Orval Kent Food Company, the country's largest manufacturer of prepared salads.

His accomplishments in these unrelated industries provide some insight into his passion and leadership skills. He also brings the same passion to his speaking where he speaks to many corporate audiences on a variety of topics, including leadership, motivation, and team building.

Mac has authored or co-authored eighteen books that have sold over three million copies. His titles include:

- Change is Good … You Go First
- Charging the Human Battery
- Customer Love
- Finding Joy
- Learning to Dance in the Rain
- 212°: The Extra Degree
- 212° Service
- Motivational Quotes
- One Choice
- The Nature of Success
- The Power of Attitude
- The Power of Kindness
- The Essence of Leadership
- The Road to Happiness
- The Dash
- To a Child, Love is Spelled T-I-M-E
- You Can't Send a Duck to Eagle School
- What's the Big Idea?

For more information about Mac, visit www.simpletruths.com

If you have enjoyed this book we invite you to check out our entire collection of gift books, with free inspirational movies, at **www.simpletruths.com.** You'll discover it's a great way to inspire **friends** and **family,** or to thank your best **customers** and **employees.**

For more information, please visit us at:
www.simpletruths.com Or call us toll free... **800-900-3427**